An Awakening

God reveals Himself

In so many different ways...

That it could take a lifetime

To realize He's been part of it!

Foolish Children

It was a very hot August in the late 50's
Seven months pregnant, she had traveled nearly all day
First on a train from Boston and then on a bus
Through an empty ugly part of New Jersey
To a place called Fort Dix, where he had finished basic training.

Their meeting was tentative - uncertain of who they were
They touched each other carefully...like strangers
He in his uniform...creased - crisp... and crew cutted
Was toned, tanned and trimmer than he'd ever been
She was heavier of course...puffed up in her pregnancy
Disheveled and distraught from her journey....

They had married a year before - it seemed like the thing to do!
He had been her only boyfriend...the first one that wanted her
And sadly enough that was sufficient criteria -
Since she thought so little of herself!
They were allowed to stay in a guest room on the base
Sleeping on a lumpy bed with stiff, cheap sheets--
She wept as he comforted her with promises of better days
Assuring her that she would come - after the baby -
To wherever it was they sent him...

A Life in
VERSE

A Life in
VERSE

❧

Ruth Young

Library of Congress Control Number:		2016917459
ISBN:	Hardcover	978-1-5245-5276-3
	Softcover	978-1-5245-5275-6
	eBook	978-1-5245-5274-9

Rev. date: 10/18/2016

To order additional copies of this book, contact:
Xlibris
1-888-795-4274
www.Xlibris.com
Orders@Xlibris.com
751793

Contents

Foreword

These are my poems about some of the things and people

That happened in my life...

They are in no particular order...because life doesn't happen in order

For me the firsts and bests were last!

Cover Artwork: original painting by Ruth Young

Surprise

To be in love at any age is amazing

Fourteen - thirty - or sixty three

But to be in love at the end of your life

Is most incredible!

It's like first love for a second time...

Passion seasoned with wisdom -

Fantasy peppered with reality

A surprise in old age...

A gift with no strings attached!

Just When

Just when I thought life

Was about growing old gracefully

And taking joy from family ...

An amazing thing happened to me

It was Donald my love!!

Two aging would-be poets

Sat next to one another

At a writers workshop one day...

And became one of God's

Small unnoticed miracles...

Happy to have found each other

After years of loneliness

And ill-fated relationships!

After the visit, alone on the train...she wept again
Not sure of why but trying not to feel the way she felt -
Overheated and exhausted, she dozed
And hoped that she was dreaming
That all of this was just a dream!

She didn't want to be going home to her parents
She didn't want to be having a baby
She didn't even want to be married...
She didn't want to be anything that she was!

For Aunt Irene on her 90th Birthday

A little girl walks on the beach
With Auntie Irene the beautiful
She takes her hand and feels a magic love
She will hold onto the rest of her life...

A nine-year old visits
With Auntie Irene the beautiful
She takes a streetcar - after school
An climbs the steep hill to Deering Castle
Where her fairy-godmother lives...
Who else could change a plain chubby child
Into a lovely princess

A teenager watches
Her Auntie Irene the role-model
The epitome of everything she wants to be
Idolized and idealized -
The perfect homemaker mother and wife

A young woman listens
To Auntie Irene the wise
With respect and admiration
Gathers her opinions seeks her advice
Every word is of value!

A middle-aged woman runs
To Auntie Irene the heart-broken
And holds her in a wrap of comfort and love -
But Irene the grief-stricken is too lost
Clouds of loneliness envelope her
As she disappears in a mist of memories...

An older woman marvels
At Irene the born-again-
Strong and new - yet with some of the old
She is handyman and philosopher
Irene of the finances - of pliers and a hammer
Of water aerobics and banana bread...

An old woman walks into the water
With aunt Irene the even older -
She takes her hand and feels the magic love
She has held onto all of her life!!

Sadness

A sidelong glance from the corner of my eye, passing a mirror
Wondering who is looking back at me...

The oppressive empty blackness of being awake at 3 A.M.
Feeling worried - not remembering quite why...

Watching those I care for stop caring for themselves -
Relationships disintegrate - lives decay beyond my control...

The hopelessness of knowing that whatever the joy the future holds
Is not equal to what the past has taken from me...

Yet I will not succumb to sadness... I am steadfast
Inexhaustible in my effort to remain alive and well!

I find tiny diamonds among the countless pebbles
Others carelessly toss away each day...

An inner force compels me from my bed-
From the warmth of dreaming - out into the world

I run another mile- finish a painting- sing a new Cantata
And I will not succumb to sadness--at least not today...

Moving in

A pair of old shoes
Stilled remained in the closet
In the corner - way back...
Forgotten or overlooked ?
Maybe left deliberately
A message that he had been there
Lived there...had other shoes
Other clothes in this very closet
Empty now except for dust...
And these old shoes!

Had he worn them to dance ?
To walk in the park
Or travel to exotic lands ?
Where had these old shoes been?
Whose feet sat next to them
At a dinner table or concert ?
Had they seen sorrow - these shoes ?
Heard laughter or had tears fall on them?
Had they danced at weddings ?
Trudged through cemeteries ?
Paced in hospital corridors ?

Who was this man
Who left his shoes ?
And why did he leave them ?
Perhaps for me - ah yes
He left them there for me!
So I will leave them
Exactly where they are
And fit my shoes around them…

Intuition

My life has been like listening

To some familiar music

On the radio...

Trying to guess the composer --

And even when

I think I've got it,

Unexpected changes

Make me just as sure

Of something else...

But I've always known when it was Mahler!!

Introspection

I dreamed my life into an empty field
Where I stand alone at twilight
Every minute closer to dark.
Nothing will grow here
The ground is putrid with decay
And the odor of my errors

I shiver in a blanket of sadness
Afraid of what is yet to come -
Despair surrounds me
And I'm paralyzed
By my own nothingness

If I can wake myself enough -
To make it towards the trees
That edge the field -
Then a new dream may appear
To carry forth another year
My aching heart!

For Don

You didn't know me before you loved me,
So you wouldn't understand
How your love has changed me!
It has made me into someone new
Different from anyone I've ever been…
You created a woman to love
The one you wanted and needed!!

So perhaps I'm just your imagination
An illusion…your favored dream
Maybe…
Maybe that's all I am!!!

For if you were to leave me
I would disappear for sure…
I cannot exist without you
Not now - Not anymore!!

He said/she said

Take me with you into your dreams -

Let me see what you see when you look at me!

Let me feel what you feel when you think of me...

Let me know what you know when we kiss!

You are the darling of my dreams -

When I see you I see the face of my future!

When I think of you I feel wrapped - up in love...

When we kiss I know I have everything!

And So It's The Magic

And so it's the magic
Of lovers through the ages
Believing they have everything...
Two lives becoming one
Fine lines merging -
But respectful of separateness
He ends where she begins -
Yet they allow differences...
Seeing the beauty of one
And the magic of both -
They are bound by togetherness...

To look in the other's heart
And see yourself there
Is truly a joy -
And to have found your one true love
Is life's greatest blessing!

Much to Learn

He has gone…
She sits on the edge of her bed
Abandoned and alone at 2:00 A.M.
Loving is so hard! - she says

Their coupling had been odd -
Unusually silent - yet too intense
And with the unwelcome presence
Of some other selves who interfere
With who they are to each other
In this moment…

She realizes there are parts of him
That she can never know or understand -
And she herself has given up
So much of who she was
To become who he loves -
That she is fragile and uncertain
In her own Identity…

He has gone…
She sits on the edge of her bed at 2:00 A.M.
Loving is so hard! - she says
And she knows
There is still much to learn!

Grandmothering

A splendid happening
The title role you never chose
Or had to be trained for...
An unimagined joy!
The purest kind of love,
Unfettered and unconditional --
Flows boundlessly
Toward your darlings of perfection,
Who grow and flourish --
As the likes of them
Become your unique pleasure!

Should you ever perceive
Some tiny flaw among them --
Easily and certainly
Attribute it to a failing
Of the parent that you didn't raise...
Or better still...
The other grandmother!

It's Over

We allowed…
The sand of love
To slip unnoticed
Through our fingers --
Over the years
Of disconcern -
Of discontent!

We allowed…
The few grains of goodness
To be washed away
In tides of anger --
Of unhappiness -
Uninvolved, uncommitted!

We could have allowed…
A pebble of kindness,
One to the other
And carried it off
Each to separate shores!

Poor Stan

With all of me so full of HIM

I cannot even find

A little corner place

Where I have put my love for you!

Some sadness sits between us on the couch

And turns itself to anger...

My poor sweetheart

Undeservedly attacked -

Just for sitting there

Not being him!

There's No one To Dance with

There's no one to dance with
Says the old lady to herself -
But I've naught to complain!

I still sing in the choir and work in the garden
I can jog and do yoga - or hike for a week…
There are dinners and concerts, book clubs and art shows,
I paint and write poems or teach someone to read…

There's no one to dance with
Says the old lady to herself -
But I've naught to complain!

I'm surrounded by people who want to be near me -
People to drink with, to eat with and talk to…
To laugh with and cry with … and sometimes hug -
But there's no one to dance with

There's no one to dance with!!

One Summer Companion

Mr. Levinson was my aunt's father-
But not my grandfather
He lived in our beach house the summer I was ten..
A smiley man - with blue eyes, one leg and crutches..
I don't remember where he slept or how he got around-
But he spent most of his time in the large sunroom
That stretched across the front of the house...

He was always there when I came home from a bike ride
Or a swim at the beach with my friends -
Always happy to see me - eager to talk or play something
He taught me checkers and gin rummy...
Tried chess, but I was never good at games!

He was the first person in my life to treat me as an adult
He talked to me as though I understood him
And listened to what I had to say as if it mattered...
We discussed what was in the newspaper,
Which he read faithfully every day -
Things about the war or President Roosevelt -
Things about the Germans and Japanese,
Concentration camps and Victory Gardens
And the great injustices of life...

But never anything personal!!
I didn't ask about his leg or why he lived with us
Or where the rest of his family were...
And he'd pretend he hadn't heard my mother yelling,
Pretend he didn't know I was spending time with him
Because I was punished and couldn't go outside...
We enjoyed each other's company -
We listened to the radio or read books together...

And then at the end of summer -
I asked him to sign my autograph book... and he wrote:
"Good luck to the next District Attorney of Plymouth County"
I didn't understand what he meant but I knew it was a compliment...

To Allan after 25 Octobers

A snip of music from the past

Snags in a corner of my heart

A vision flashes ... a tear almost forms

Old people in love watch each other

In a way that stings my eyes

Envy consumes me ... I can hardly breath

What a disappointment you are!!

To have left me like this - all these years

Without love - without romance - without you!

To Allan After 30 years

I have never let you go
I have kept you in mind
And held you in my heart
These many empty loveless years…
I've heard your voice ten thousand times
And felt your boundless love.
You have spoken in my dreams
Inspired me… urged me…
Cheered me through sadness
And kept me from my worst self.
You've whispered patience in my ear,
Tapped kindness on my heart -
And all this time you've been watching me!

I saw you at the lake where we were walking---
A cardinal appeared as we took each other's hands
So I knew that you were there…hovering near…
To watch our miracle unfold.
And so it has---And now you know
I am loved again…I can let you go!!

On Being Bernie's Friend

Being Bernie's friend was not always easy
He expected a lot!

We had to be ready on time - or earlier
And walk a little faster than we'd like
To a place we weren't sure we wanted to go...

Or we had to ride in his car, holding hands
With our mouths and our eyes closed!
To one of his favorite restaurants...

We ate what he thought was best for us
And declined another drink or a dessert
When he said we shouldn't have it!

Being Bernie's friend was not always easy
He set a hard example and made us measure up!
He watched out for us.....took care of us
And had our best interest at heart!

Being Bernie's friend was not always easy
But we loved it --- and we loved him!
He made us our best selves ...
How can we be without him ?

To David After He Died

I wish we could have met
Just one more time...
Pulled out a few good memories
Been a little kind to each other

But it couldn't be
You had to keep your pride
I understand that now!

We stayed together far too long -
I out of loyalty and owe-ness
You for what you called love...
We didn't know how
To make each other happy!

I couldn't be who you thought I was,
And I never really knew who you were...
What a waste - a sad waste of life - and time!

No Indictment

"I'm profoundly disappointed"
Said Michael Brown's mother today
And I'm sure that she is....As I am!!
Disappointed in a system that doesn't work -
Infuriated by a system that mocks justice!

A diseased system
Infected with the killing of young blacks -
One yesterday in Cleveland
Another last week in New York...
Someone...someplace last month
Last year and two years ago -
Ten years...twenty years
It's always been there - a chronic infection-
Rampant inequality on the rise!

How can we stop it - who is there to stop it ?
Surely not me!!
I am heartbroken and ashamed
But I can do nothing!
All these years I have done nothing!
The "bleeding heart" liberal
The "change the world" woman
Of the sixties and seventies
Was too busy in her wonderful white life
To do anything!

I hear the cries of a hundred black men
Seeking justice from the grave...
Their deaths are on my conscience
I have done nothing

But today I am a black woman...
And my outrage is unspeakable!
My pain is unbearable
For I am a grandmother to them all!

The Other Self

Each day is a constant battle

To know who I am

I'm always aware of the other self...

Because I have to be...

She tries to take charge of my life!

Particularly when I'm anxious or conflicted

She will take over

Spoil the moment - say the wrong thing

And steal the best from me!

Her agenda is selfishness and control

Not just over me but of those I love!

I have to watch her all the time

And monitor her plans...

Reminding her who is in charge

Or else she might destroy me...

Take a risk

Take a risk and embrace a dream

Trust yourself to change your life...

God will help you

He has given you the means

He has sent you the answer!

Maybe

A foolish teenger…
She says to the wrinkles in the mirror -
An old lady behaving like a teenager!
With butterflies in her stomach
Waiting for an email…

It's nonsense sheer nonsense!
She says to the wrinkles in the mirror -
And then she makes a list -
Reasons why she shouldn't want him
Then another longer one
For him not wanting her!

But something has happened -
She tells the wrinkles in the mirror
Some kind of magic or miracle
Made an old lady young again!

There are feelings not ready for words -

And maybe…just maybe - she says
Maybe he can dance!!

A Small Miracle

He was the love-mate of her heart

There from its first beat...

So strange he didn't find her

And she never thought to look for him

Until it was almost too late!

But she came one day

To sit beside him at a workshop

In the one seat left for her...

Divine plan or happenstance?

It doesn't matter- for in that moment

There was purposeful order

In a world of random chaos

And thus they became Don and Ruth

One of God's small miracles

When grandma was a little girl

When grandma was a little girl
She didn't have a cell phone
Or an IPOD or TV
Instead she had a radio...
And she sat there every day
Listening to her programs…
Jack Armstrong, Superman
Wonder woman and Tom Mix-
In the evening the whole family
Sat together and listened to the radio
The news was on and there was always music
Sometimes a story or a play
A talk by the President - Lux Radio Theatre
The voices came from the radio
But the pictures were in grandma's head....

When grandma was a little girl
She didn't go on playdates
She just went downstairs to the street -
There were always girls outside
Jumping rope or playing hopscotch
Sometimes Hide and seek...
She went shopping with her mother -
No mall- no supermarkets
Just rows of little stores along the avenue
A meat market - the bakery
A drug store and a five and ten.
If they bought more than they could carry,
A boy would bring it later- in a carton
On a specially made bicycle.

When Grandpa was a little boy

When grandpa was a little boy
He didn't have a computer
Nintendo or a gameboy
There was no peewee soccer or T-ball
Instead he played in an empty lot
With neighborhood kids
And whatever stuff
They could come up with...
Sometimes he played marbles
On a patch of dirt with a hole in the ground.
He had shooters and aggies
Which he kept in a drawstring pouch -
His mother made on her sewing machine.

When grandpa was a little boy
He walked to school
To a brick building three streets away
No Playground or ball field
Just a brick schoolyard with a tall iron fence
At recess the gates were locked...
He played dodgeball, red rover and tag
When the bell rang, everyone lined-up
Two by two - class by class
The class with the straightest lines
Carried the flag inside...
Grandpa loved the sound of the teacher's heels

Clicking on the bricks as she walked
Back and forth examining the lines.
How wonderful when the sounds came close
And she handed him the flag!

Figure It Out

He needs approval
But she gives affection
He showers her with compliments
While she craves caresses!
Each doing for the other
What they want for themselves
Living what they think love means!

Every now and then it stops working
So they talk about it...
Saying hurtful things to one another
Sleeping with resentment
And waking up to sadness!

"Is love how I feel for you?" she asks
"Or is it how I make you feel?"
He says he doesn't know
But they'll figure it out...
And their lives go on -
Only a little changed.

Rhody and Jack

The door swung open
The one between the dining room and kitchen
That went both ways and caught her by surprise!
She jumped back from peeking through the crack
And they just stood looking at each other...
The door had swung open!

He was the cousin of her sister's girlfriend -
Invited to the party she was too young to attend!
And came with his brother from the other end of town
He didn't like soda or punch - said it was too sweet
So he'd come to the kitchen for a drink of water
The door had swung open!

They spoke about their lives and families
Shared their hopes and plans for the future...
And within an hour their love story had begun!
They exchanged their hearts...
The door had swung open
And it didn't close for seventy-five years!!

Love Story Part One

A young woman stands at the window
She is watching her neighbor mow his lawn.
She is twenty - four… already a wife and mother
And she is falling in love for the first time!

She can't explain what it feel like to look at him -
But she knows it's like nothing she's ever felt
Passionately out of control - she feels dirty..sneaky
She hides behind the curtain - ashamed of herself
For watching him …. For wanting him

They're together a lot these two ---
With husbands and wives, mingling with neighbors
Children playing in each others plastic pools
"Fifties" couples… flirting, grilling hot dogs
Drinking martinis in connecting backyards…

But she never drinks and she doesn't flirt
She only tries to be near him…to look at him
His touch is electric - she feels her skin sizzle!
She blushes if they speak…embarrassed it my show -
The yearning is so enormous…It just might show!

And of course he's seen it - or hopes he has -
For he too holds a secret love for her....
But time passes unhappily for both of them....
Locked in their unbearable marriages
Each one's pain and longing unknown to the other...
Unexpressed and unacceptable to such decent people
Such repressed and moral people!!

One day they are alone - he puts his hands on her shoulders
"You know" he says....and quickly she covers his mouth
So the unspeakable is not spoken --
And nothing changes between them for many many years!

Love Story Part Two

She divorces,relocates and remarries
As good friends, they stay in touch…
She embraces his wife's friendship
As the thread that ties them together.

When she relocates nearer to him
They begin to see a lot of each other -
First as couples meeting for dinner…
Then as friends who meet secretly for lunch.

He pulls himself from the shambles of an ugly marriage,
While she easily - perhaps callously - walks out of hers…
She won't let a mere eight - year relationship
Keep her from a dream she's nurtured more than twenty!!
They live together in a state of bliss and wonder
Feeling loved in a way that neither ever imagined possible!

And then they marry…but he is already sick!
They marry as if the act can make him well…
She believes that if she loves him enough, he will get better
She is unable to see him deteriorate…

Thoughts While Growing Old

Every great thinker studies the philosophy of the ages
In order to come up with his own thoughts...
Every composer listens to the music of the masters
In order to find his own special combination of notes...
Every great writer reads and absorbs his favorites
In order to develop his own unique talent...

None of us is original!
We are not born with thoughts, music or poetry in our heads...
It is what we make of what we learn
And what we choose to be our influences...
Life experiences shape our thoughts,
Learning refines our talent...
Openness to new ideas develops creativity!
The thinker must always process new thoughts
The composer always be listening -
And the writer must read!

We can never let ourselves get old and stale -
To become cynical and tired of the world
Is an insult to the purpose of our lives!
We can never say we know all when we want to know
And that we don't read or listen
Because there is nothing we can learn!

Arrogance is destructive- it diminishes our creativity
Every day can be a lesson-
An opportunity to look inside
And change something about ourselves
That in some way may provide new understanding
A practice in patience and tolerance..
A chance to give and grow -
To love and trust and be part of the world!

Scared

Totally vulnerable -

Completely exposed…

Their naked hearts

Cry out to one another

Begging for trust!!

Locked In

Locked in an almost impossible dream,

He fails to grasp the miracle he's living in

And takes only part of it for his own...

Bound by vestiges of compulsion,

He is driven by needs no longer necessary

And is blinded by false visions of his life!

The turmoil is of his own making

For the truth is right before him...

But his eyes have not yet seen

What his heart already knows!

Nursing him herself, she feeds and kisses - hold and bathes
And when he is no more than a skeleton,
She cradles him in her arms - and thinks -
Tomorrow will bring a miracle
But it doesn't and he dies

Devastated and inconsolable, she can't let him go
They waited so long for so little...
It isn't fair - she thinks - some cruel kind of joke
Or perhaps her punishment!
She took another woman's husband
And broke her darlings heart...

And for this she pays the rest of her life
With sadness and longing and never-ending grief.

On Accepting Change

I turn off the phone
I have been talking to my niece about thanksgiving-
It will be at her house this year instead of mine
And some of my family will not be there…
"things change " she tells me "our family has changed
Grown - spread out..we need to include etc. blah blah"
I say okay - I'll do whatever you want
But I am heartbroken - I am giving up something
That has mattered to me for a very long time…
I am accepting change which means I've grown old
And cannot do what I want to do or be who I was!

I sit at the concert
I am listening to the choir in which I sang for 12 years
Retired now I am in the audience instead of on the stage-
Looking at the spot where I used to stand
Fills me with sadness and a sense of loss…
"things change" he told me "older singers should step aside
Make room for younger eager better voices"
I said okay - I'll do whatever you want
But I was heartbroken at giving up something
That had mattered to me for a very long time…
I am accepting change which means I've grown old
And cannot do what I want to do or be who I was!

What's next ?
A bleak future full of change?
The wrinkles deepen and the knees weaken
I'll say okay - I'll do whatever you want
And I will give up one by one
All the things that matter to me
Not do what I want to do or be who I was!
Maybe better to change it all at once
I could just give up now

But No - I think NOT YET!
As long as I'm running in the streets
And posing on my yoga mat
Nothing can change…
I will do what I want and be who I am
One day at a time - in love with my life
Change will wait

The BabySitter

Rose Sullivan was my babysitter
She appeared shortly after my brother was born,
Arriving every Saturday afternoon with a small red suitcase
In which she carried plaid pajamas, metal curlers
And her Sunday morning church clothes
I loved her instantly...she had come to be with me!
To play with me, give me supper and put me to bed.
In the morning, I dashed from my room
To find her on the living room couch...
Sleeping soundly with the curlers in her hair
She was always happy to see me - glad to be awake for early Mass
I would help her get dressed...fastening nylon stockings to a garter belt -
Zipping a skirt or buttoning a blouse.
She let me unroll the curlers and brush her hair...

And when she was ready... the very last thing she did
Was look in the bathroom mirror and put on a small amount
Of the most beautiful pink lipstick I had ever seen
I watched her so intently...so longingly
That one day she turned and quickly dabbed my mouth -
"Don't tell!" she said and left for church.
Standing on the toilet, alone in the mirror - I examined myself
Blond hair like hers.....blues eyes - like hers
And now with that bit of pink lipstick!
For the next few hours or so - until my mother wiped it off
I thought I was Rose Sullivan

Thank You Aunt Irene

Thank you for staying alive
Until I got there to say goodbye
And tell you I love you -
Yet another time…

Thank you for letting me hold you
And for smiling at my kisses!
For knowing me - saying my name
And telling me I'm beautiful

Thank you for being able to give me
In last few hours of your life -
The same love and attention
I have always needed from you!!

Thank you for it all!
For everything you've given me -
Done for me or been to me…
Thank you my wonderful Aunt Irene!!

I Saw You This Morning

I think I saw you this morning…
You were walking towards me
As I came back over the bridge
To meet me halfway -
As you often did

I think I saw you this morning…
You were in the front yard
"Deadheading" my geraniums
And weeding the rock garden -
As you often did

I think I saw you this morning…
You were on my little porch
Sitting in the rocking chair
Drinking your coffee -
As you often did

I know I saw you this morning…
You were at the breakfast table
Looking up smiling
When I came through the door -
As you have always done

Memory Of My Mother

What did mother give me ?
I really don't know - I mean I'm not sure
Or it's hard to remember...

I spent most of my childhood trying to get free of her
Did she keep me too close - hold me too tight ?
Did she need me too much ? Maybe

I was always outside or at other kids houses
Establishing my freedom - my separateness from her
Determined not to be like her, I kept my distance
And I was unaware of who she was...

Most of my life I played the "proper daughter"
Maintaining a superficial closeness
Allowing her the joy of grandmotherhood
And caring for her at the end of her life...

Sitting at her funeral
Listening to what friends and family said of her
I was stunned at their extolled virtues -
Startled by the praise heaped upon this woman
Who did not sound at all like my mother
But rather more like me
Looking into the mirror now
I see her looking back at me -
If I did not become my mother
I somehow just absorbed her...

Memory Of My Father

What did my father give me ? Very little --
Not many hugs and few accolades of praise or love...
Only the need to excel at whatever I did
That's what my father gave me!

Maybe at first it was so he'd take notice
Like me better ... pay some attention
I always had to be the best or one of the best...
From second grade through graduate school
I pushed myself and I was!

Thriving on my own excellence, I looked for it in others
Expecting it from colleagues - and exacting it from students
I was not always popular in my career...
"Too tough" They'd say... "You can't please her!"
It was hard to be my husband or even my friend
Harder to be my son or grandchild!

Now the old woman - still demanding of herself-
I sit in the corner of the yoga class
The oldest.... trying to be one of the best
And I realize that what little my father gave me
THOUGH I DON'T THANK HIM FOR IT
Has shaped my life!

Black Women

I see black women
How splendid they are!
Born with a pride and graciousness
White women can only imitate...
I see the young girl looking at her life
With freshness and enthusiasm...
She is joyous and optimistic
Hoping for things white girls take for granted.
I see black women of all ages embracing each other
In friendship, with camaraderie and compassion
Beyond what white women know...
I see them support and cheer each other,
Connecting at a level of closeness
White women don't understand...

I see black women aging with dignity -
They know who they are!
Centuries of sorrow and suffering
Carved the furrows in their cheeks...
Generations of injustice
Are the wrinkles on their hands!
They age with wisdom and passion
They know who they are!
Their mothering and grandmothering
Convey a message
To the daughters and granddaughters
Who will one day understand and absorb
The importance of their being!!

And You Phyllis

And you Phyllis...
Always insisting there was a Heaven and God and love
Telling me you would send me a sign and let me know
That you were right - but you never have!
Joking in those days of dying - about death itself
About being bald and boobless and flirting
With old men in the nursing home…
Never being afraid - always laughing at life!

And you Phyllis…
Even before that,in the time we spent together
After Phil died - year after year on the Outer banks
Always the same conversations -over and over again
God and Heaven and true love!!
With all the discussions and arguments
You never changed my view - even a little -
Nor I yours

And you Phyllis
Popping into my mind the other day
When I saw the little yellow wildflowers -
The ones you called "scrambled eggs"
Growing in my favorite spot along the harbor road -
A place similar to one of our childhood ..
Where we rode our bikes and climbed on rocks
And talked about all those things that mattered to you ….
God and Heaven and true love!

And you Phyllis
Always insisting there was a Heaven and God and love
And being right! You had been right all along …..
I understood that - standing in my favorite spot -
It is I who just found out!
A man came into my life- taught me of Heaven
Brought me to God and gave me true love …
I was wanting to tell you all about him -
Then looking down at those "scrambled egg" flowers
I realized you already knew!!

Waiting

The hardest thing we do in life
Is wait!
And oh how much waiting we do
Have done … will do!
Hours of anxiousness
And loss of patience…
Waiting for good things
Bad things as well…
Waiting for happiness
Unhappiness too…sometimes

We wait for the right person
We wait for love -
Wait for a child to be born
To grow - up and marry
We wait to be grandparents
Wait for our own parents
To die…

And all the while
We are spending lifetimes
Of waiting
In supermarket lines
And at airports!
In the offices of our Doctor
Lawyer - Dentist - Accountant

We wait for important phone calls
Something special in the mail
The furniture delivery
The repairman that never comes

We wait
The world moves along
And yet we wait
Still wait.. Will wait
For our own inevitable demise …

On Being Apart

I'm startled by the silence

In the absence of your breathing!

And I miss my own good sleep

In our own good bed

Where some part of me

Is always touching you....

Communication

They dance around each other's words

He doesn't say quite what he's thinking -

So she hears what she'd like him to be thinking

And waltzes through the day with misconception -

Which he later dispels - he thought she understood!

He gets a little angry - she gets a little hurt...

It's their routine!

And once again

The world shrinks in around them

A little bit more!

Just Us

We must banish from our life

Intruding past selves

And ghosts of those

Who did or didn't love us...

They offend who we are now!!

We blend in our togetherness

Making each other

Beautiful and strong

The future can shape our love

If the past no longer owns us!

Our Angels

In the world of believe
Or make believe (if you prefer)
Anything is possible!
There is a Heaven and of course a God
Who assigns teams of angels
To do His work on earth!

And so sit Allan and Dorothy (co - workers of a sort)
On the edge of a cloud observing their project -
Congratulating each other on their accomplishment
So pleased with themselves they are!!

Dorothy: They really do look good together don't they ?
           I see why people are saying that!
Allan: Yes, they're beautiful and happy too!
           But I never thought we could do it...
           They were both difficult in their own way!
Dorothy: Tough choice...such an odd combination
           It was a challenging assignment
           More than once I thought we'd lost them

Allan: Defiant and defensive
           He wouldn't listen!
           It took all my patience
           To make him hear
           What I needed to tell him

Dorothy: Uncertain and insecure
        She often wanted to run
        It took all my strength
        To hold her back
        And keep her in my house!

Allan: But we did it...made our miracle
         How changed they are!
         And they've learned so much…

Dorothy: Love was their teacher
         They changed for each other -
Allan: So we brought them together
         This unlikely pair -
Dorothy: Because they are the ones
         That God chose for us!!

Allan: Him to cherish and care for her
         As I would have done
Dorothy: Her to be the mother and grandmother
         That I would have been

         Do they know our part in this ?
         No, they say it's God's plan…
         And it is really!
         We just mind the details!!

Thank You

Thank you Dorothy for finding me…

Coming into my life and making it your own!

And sharing such joy and love with me

As I never would have known!!

Don and Ruth

It's strange that they ever met at all
These two...such an unlikely pair..
A self described "Ghetto Rat" -
And an "Ivy League" lady!
Destiny put them next to each other,
Two would be poets,
At a workshop in the library -
On a wednesday afternoon...

And they each brought to that moment
An enormous need and hunger -
Yet to be revealed...for each other!
So astonished by their feelings...
And delighted with each other - they fell in love...
And amazed themselves with with joy and pleasure
The like of which neither can can remember
Having known before!

And they'll never take for granted
The blessings of their togetherness -
They are ever thankful for each other
But especially to God!
Whose presence in their lives
They now acknowledge
As the miracle they have become

Divorce is Hereditary

A small boy sits up in bed in the middle of the night
Startled by the arguing of his parents through the wall
It's not the first time and this time it seems worse
The intensity of the anger the shrillness of the voices
Makes him feel weak and sick to the stomach...
He is frightened because he knows it's over!
There will be a divorce and life will never be the same
He curls up in a ball and cries...Will he survive ??
He does...he manages...he learns

He blocks his ears to the rantings of the mother
And waits patiently between the visits of the father
Who sometimes shows up but more frequently postpones or cancels
The car show, the fishing trip, the shopping for the catcher's mitt
He learns to live with disappointment
He manages divorce!

He grows up telling himself from time to time
That he will never marry
Never bring a child into a loveless ugly world!
But as nature would have it, he looks for love
And marries the wrong woman...
They have a son whom he cherishes
And tries ever so hard to protect
From what he fears the future may hold...
But he doesn't...because he can't!
And some years later he leaves a small boy
In the middle of the night curled up in a ball
Crying in bed
Divorce is hereditary

Diamond In The Rough,

Oh my God...Don't tell me he's dead!
Said the fiancee' of Philando
To the policeman who had shot him

They were stopped for a "busted" tail light
And Philando is dead!
They did everything they were asked to do
But Philando is dead!!
They knew how to act - they were prepared
Such incidents are a way of life for them
Yet Philando is dead!!

He did nothing wrong and was not a criminal
Quite the contrary...he was a gentle caring man
But he's dead...Philando dead -
Another tragic killing of an innocent black man!!

And Diamond's life is shattered
Her child's future is changed
Her loved one is gone...She is heartbroken!

I want to share her pain and understand her grief…
But more than that I am outraged and angry beyond belief
By the repeated killing of black men
Who are fathers, sons, brothers, husbands, and fiancee's

I suspect Diamond loved her black man
As much as I love mine!
Who, thank God is not a police statistic -
Although he could be

Our Shame

Another injustice - another tragedy!
It just goes on and on
City after city - week after week
Police shooting innocent black men!!
Some say the situation is getting better
But truth be told - it's not
The chasm is ever - widening
And will continue to do so
Until we agree on the real issues…
Acknowledge the truth - accept facts!!

Nothing can change until
The decision makers and politicians
Admit that there is a problem
And choose to address it!

Nothing will change until
We stop dismissing slavery
As long - forgotten history
And suffer its shame!

It is the shame of our heritage
That those who came to escape persecution
Later become the persecutors
And built their fortunes for generations
By enslavement and the fruit it bore…